Baihu Fāng 西方白虎方
& Pier Pia Paul Zellin

AF188507

ZERO
MEDITATION

No need to meditate –
life happens anyway !

E X T E N D E D EDITION
*including beach yoga poetry
and new articles from 2019*

Paul Zellin, born January 6, 1947 in New York, he was a worldwide renowned wisdom teacher of the Human Potential Movement in San Francisco until the eighties. Now living anonymously in Tamalpais Valley running a restaurant for his *No Yoga Food* company.

Pia & Pier Zellin, born as twins September 9, 1974 in Berlin. Their father Paul Zellin forced them as children to meditate (spiritual abuse). Since 2014 Pier worked as press spokesman for the *League of Empty Ones (LDL)*. In October 2015 he moved to his sister to Cape Town (South Africa) where Pia still teaches *Anti Yoga*. Since 2017 they commute between Berlin, Cape Town and Bay Area (San Francisco).

Baihu Fāng 西方白虎方 (real name Peter Zellin), born December 6, 1947 in New York. Working as web designer for the german *LDL* group of former gurus of the spiritual scene. Practising *Null Yoga* (founded by nephew Pier & niece Pia). Living as a freelance artist (experimental videos and digital photography) at Venice Beach, L.A. (California) since 1975.

THE LEAGUE OF EMPTY ONES was founded 2014 in Germany as an anonymous transspiritual network of former gurus that became politically involved. Its purpose was fulfilled in 2018 by writing the german N.A.Z.I.-BRANDBRIEF.

www.zeroyoga.de

9 783746 074900

ZERO MEDITATION, 2018
ISBN 9783746074900 (ORIGINAL)
© EXTENDED NEW EDITION 2019
Manufacturing and publisher: BoD
Books on Demand, Norderstedt, Germany

*"I have no other self
than the totality of things
of which I am aware."*

*"Trying to define yourself is like
trying to bite your own teeth."*

*"The meaning of life
is just to be alive. It is
so plain and so obvious
and so simple. And yet,
everybody rushes around
in a great panic as if
it were necessary
to achieve something
beyond themselves."*

Alan Watts
January 6, 1915 (England) –
November 16, 1973 (California)

This 5th book titled *"ZERO MEDITATION: NO NEED TO MEDITATE – LIFE HAPPENS ANYWAY!"* by the so-called League of Empty Ones (LDL) contains all the original english articles that were published for the german projects

www.urruhe.de &
www.nullyoga.de

between 2015 and 2019 about a new kind of transspirituality that defines the whole life as enlightened instead of single persons. Wisdom is therefore no longer a special knowledge within an individual brain but a general *"happeness"* between all elements of the infinite universe.

© EmojiArt.de by Tanja Lulu Play Nerd

As soon as *"the seer of nothingness"* disappears, also nothingness disappears. It was just the last *"holy"* projection of the ego. No ego, no emptiness. Beyond emptiness the infinity of reality starts to be felt as absolute itself. Now and now and now. Nowing instead of knowing :-)

NO NEED TO DO ANY YOGA. WE DO ZERO YOGA: *"ZEROYOGA"*. BE PART OF A WORLDWIDE BRAND-NEW MOVEMENT – START STOPPING YOGA! EVERY MOMENT IS YOGA!

Let yourself be distracted by anybody and anything in your surrounding in order not to meditate! Never meditate!
Enjoy ZERO YOGA XL :-)

To be AWAKE means: there is no more dualistic paradox. You ARE what you are. You DO what you do. Everything IS absolute. This is *"ZERO YOGA"!*

NO IMAGINATION – REALITY IS ENOUGH!

How can you be NOT *"connected"* to the stream of life as you ARE a part of it? You need not *"connect"*, you are WITHIN anyway :-) So you can never *"sleep"*. ANYTHING you do is awake!

Zeroyoga is the opposition of Zenyoga. By practising Zenyoga you must be DOUBLE MINDFUL while the masters of Zeroyoga do NOT MIND at all :-)

THERE IS: No true enlightened self. No self at all. No direct experience of God. No god at all. YOU ARE ALRIGHT WITHOUT RELIGIOUS NEEDS!

The direct experience of reality is absolute. Nothing else but reality is IT.

Don't wait for the ocean, life IS the ocean! You are a wave! FLOW!

A limited soul is afraid of the BIG BOREDOM without any sense, so it needs illusions like reason and progress to be permanently occupied with itself. But there are no tests for growing, reality is absolutely fulfilled in every single moment the way it is: PAIN IS PAIN AND PEACE IS PEACE!

FROM HEARTBEAT TO HORIZON: INFINITE I !

ZEROYOGA doesn't transform you neither inside nor outside. YOU ARE just the complete reality that happens without any difficulty: EASY YOGA!

New Spirituality is same psychotic as any other religious system that makes you believe in transcendental illusions!

THERE IS NO EGO BUT
TOTAL MOVEMENT...

FEELING (by) MEANS (of) FLOWING...

Not your EGO is an illusion but GOD who is just a thought of your EGO to disidentify from the WORLD that is our ABSOLUTE REAL paradise!

FEEL COMPLETE / NO SPIRITUAL NEED / YOUR HEARTBEAT IS / NATURAL HEAT

Avoid *"digital burnout"* by reaching your SPIRITUAL BURNOUT first! Don't stick to religious hope of finding God — FIND YOURSELF AWARE OF NOW!

NO BURNOUT WITHOUT EGO! DON'T TRY TO HEAL YOUR SO-CALLED BURNOUT BUT GET RID OF YOUR ILLUSIONARY EGO-BALLOON! YOUR NATURAL i IS IN FLOW!

Mindfulness is an egocentric bullshit! There's no need to be mindful as there's simply nobody to be anything at all. EVERYTHING IS ANYWAY! Everything is existential now. Everything is really what it simply is right now. Give reality a chance to be!

Practising Nullyoga means to feel fulfilled in every moment/movement. NO RELIGIOUS NEEDS: RESPECT HAPPENS! We are 1 family!

As long as you believe in anything you cannot be nondually PRESENT as the absolute mOMent is totally free of any belief – no psychic terror!

Nullyoga feels sorry for people that get hurt or killed thru terror bombing but also for those SICK SOULS that believe in brutality.

It's no paradox! What is *"there"*, is NOT *"not"* but really absolutely HERE. But: 100% interdepending from each other...

There is no *"better you"* and no law at all neither of attraction nor energy exchange

–   vOMit your attached extra-ego and get in touch!

You must, you shall, you need, you want, if you start, if you practise – if, if, if, you, you, you MUST NOT MUST AT ALL 'cause you are it right now as i!

Your i is the only thing that you can feel from inside of yourself but it is no *"thing"* but EVERYTHiNG YOUR SENSES TOUCH!!

As long as you search for any greater truth than reality you stick to the idea of a level beyond the world, an object before big bang etc pp

Reality itself is the only truth you can find honestly. Your ego as an illusion of your thoughts belongs to this complete reality as well!

If you believe in an *"experience of nothingness"* as the nondual pole of truth, you are still an ego that separates infinity in two sides!

So-called *"integral"* people still believe in God and so-called *"non-dual"* people seek for silence.

A stupid idea of esoterical people is the so-called *"oneness"* combined with the belief that separation is an illusion. It is much easier!

Believing in yourself as a so-called person means to separate an inside from an outside object. But all things create each other right now!

A self-person is the same result of consciousness as all other objects. The REAL person does not consist of an eternal ego-core but INFINITY.

INFINITY is neither a scientific theory nor a meditation method but just the experience of your senses if you dare to be in absolute touch!

There is no different so-called *"divine"* truth behind or beyond reality that can be called God or nothingness. Non-duality happens totally NOW...

THERE IS no enlightenment, no awakening, no awareness, no non-duality, no liberation, no mindfulness to consume: NO PERSON to get rid of!

The spiritual problem is not being separated from the others but from yourself! Return to the absolute concrete SELF-FEELING: blood, breath!

If you allow yourself to BE whatever your senses experience, all other objects are ok as well because NO PERSON feels separated any longer!

INFINITY can not be separated in two sides (inside/outside, matter/meta-physics) but consists of everything reflecting each other right now!

If you believe that life would be an illusion or even just the dream of God, you are separated from THIS TOTAL MOMENT of absolute zeroness!

Infinity has got no dualistic opposite: Everything reflects each other on the one & only same infinite level called universe doing Nullyoga!

The ego wants to be something different than infinity. It is a *"cramp of conscious-ness"!* Infinity is neither full nor empty but EXISTENCE...

Zeroness is the simple fact that infinity has got no dualistic opposite! Therefore your senses touch the absolute truth flowing HERE & NOW...

As infinity has got no opposite it is neither empty nor full but just what it is: the COMPLETE BEING in the way you are aware of it today...

How can you seek for non-duality? As long as there is that seeking person you never understand that you experience non-duality all the time!

Stop believing that your ego is more than just a thought and feel that thinking itself is same infinite as the reflected object called WORLD.

Even your thinking itself is just a reflected object of your awareness and therefore a part of the infinite world without transcendental god.

As any object (your thinking itself inclu- ded!) is part of infinity it is irrelevant to call reality illusion or truth:
it is nondually (T)HERE!

Consciousness itself belongs to infinity as well as all other reflected objects of that object called *"consciousness"*.
ZERO TRANSCENDENCE...

THIS IS THE INFINITE NATURE.

THERE IS NO *"NATURE"* BEYOND THE INFINITE NATURE ITSELF. NATURE CONSISTS OF ALL EMPTY OBJECTS THAT OBSERVE EACH OTHER. EMPTINESS IS NO OBJECT AT ALL.

Society is sick: people don't trust their senses because everything is in flow. They seek for silence beyond movement instead of BEING NOW...

Did i mention enough THE IMPORTANCE OF INFINITY as a basic experience of fucking normal awareness without super-ego? Don't practise any method to get rid of your ego to be enlightened. As long as you NEED your ego you cannot wake up anyway. JUST TRUST & WAIT...

To wake up simply means to understand that THERE IS NOBODY to wake up but just your empty existence that was born and will die. That's LIFE!

Nullyoga is neither nihilism nor atheism because there is no person to BELIEVE in so-called *"nothingness"* or *"no-god"*. LIFE needs no idea!

Although Nullyoga feels TOTALLY NEUTRAL about meaningless life, it is an attitude to say completely YES. Not to something special but BEING!

So-called *"unconditioned love"* is same esoterical bullshit as the belief in non-duality: we ARE separated beings, that's how we cOMmunicate!

But BEING ITSELF is an infinite process of 1 totality that is empty within itself. Therefore everything is ABSOLUTELY connected without back.

I LOVE COMMUNICATION! I LOVE TO BE MYSELF! I LOVE TO BE A MOUTH TO TALK AND KISS! I LOVE TO BE TWO HANDS TO EMBRACE YOU! I LOVE TO BE BEING!

Every day is the best day of your life IF it wasn't yesterday or tomorrow. But it doesn't matter what is best IF you accept what happens.

It happened to me being involved into the german spiritual scene to understand that they are all stressed with the pressure of practising...

The spiritual seekers try to reach a so-called inner peace freedom love emptiness because SOMEBODY feels separated from SOMETHING. Silly!!!

As soon as that *"somebody"* reaches the goal called emptiness it happens that NOBODY is left to feel that everything IS an empty river anyway.

The river is not empty because of missing water but because the water is not frozen but FLOWING: dancing drops of the ocean called BEING...

Religions are like frozen water: people imagine that the whole infinite stream of being could be caught in an idea called God or Gaia. Silly!

As soon as the so-called *"soul"* gets empty there is nobody to feel himself naked. To BE means conscious clothing.

NO BUDDHA NO CRY

BE IDENTICAL:
GREEN IS JUST GREEN AND
NOTHING ELSE BUT GREEN

When you look into the ocean, what do you think? Oh, God made this all? Or: there must be a beginning of it all? Or: the colour is just a psychic projection and not the absolute truth? Or maybe: water is more than the element we see? The *"real"* water is behind or beyond the experienced water? You stupid idiot search for MORE than THERE IS because you did not learn to FEEL THE EMPTY INFINITY OF IT ALL! Stop thinking about the ocean and enjoy the absolute nondual truth that EVERTHING IS JUST EVERYTHING – EVERYTHING IS ITSELF !!! Everything does itself... There is no source, no essence, no god, no reason, no big bang, no absolute object that gives you any answer WHAT & WHY life IS – life just IS: zooming deep into the details of the elements you find emptiness and infinity as well as far away in universe! Microcosmos is the same as macrocosmos – green IS green, water IS water, emptiness IS emptiness, ego IS ego, love IS love – but nothing is *"more"* (on another dimension or level or other bullshit) than what it is. There is no answer but existence itself.

WINGS & WISDOM

Liberation is just a trendy spiritual mind-fuck because LIFE NEEDS NO LIBERATION at all! Who wants to be liberated from what? Just your ego believes to be in a cage but indeed there is no outside or inside of truth and your ego itself is just an illusion produced by language. LIFE ITSELF IS ABSOLUTE TRUE. The cage is just an hypnotic fantasy of your ego illusion that produces an imaginary ideal area called *"beyond"* (that is God for religious people and nothingness for new spiritual seekers). So there is neither wrong nor true liberation because there is nobody to be liberated from anything. Life is an empty butterfly itself (you are the wings of IT!) – an incredible infinite white elephant (you are the wisdom of IT!)...

IT HAPPENS (ANYWAY)

After all the EMPTY BODY ITSELF IS AWARE OF IT ALL, doesn't matter if it's called i or you. Body IS absolute. Body is the mystery. Because it is empty but *"there"*. Only spiritual seekers want to get rid of an i as a mindful opposite of a stupid iful wrong emptiness. There is no difference at all between body, i and emptiness. These are just psychotic intellectual problems. Let your i think because it is made for thinking. Let your emptiness be empty because it is made for being empty. And let your body fuck because it is made for making love! Let it all happen! IT DOES ANYWAY.

FLOW LINE

Gurus like to tell you fairy tales about awakening: You shall not look AT the void but FROM its point of view. But as long as there is somebody to look from somewhere, there is no void but still separation. The *"real"* void happens beyond both matter and void – it is the loss of the looker himself. Now there is no more void because THE void became really damn empty. Everything starts to appear as its own empty suchness, even the infinite ego points of the identity flow line playing the looking game!

PRAYER FOR DAILY NOTHINGNESS

i am not empty enough to be filled up
with the kingdom of light
i am not holy to be grounded
in love and peace
i am not enlightened to see
the truth beyond darkness
i am not awaken to understand
more than depression
i am neither insane nor in sense
of the whole
i am neither complete nor complaining
about incompleteness
i am not the person you wish
to say that it is because
i am not anybody at all
i am even not nothing
i need no more name no more face
no more prayer for life
i am the pure human being that is
conscious about its consciousness
i am no i but my eyes to see
i am no why but my wow to agree
i am no longer shy
so i don't need to flee
i am what it is and i feel that bliss
to be able to stop
that prayer of nothingness

NO...W

Tomorrow is everything to come. Now is just what did arrive for real. And yesterday will be what you wanted to come but never arrived AND what happens now. But now IS always tomorrow and yesterday AND what was now now. You are never anywhere else but now, tomorrow and yesterday at once. The problem is not the time but the YOU that wants to be SOMEWHERE. The truth is there is no *"you"* to be found at ANY time, so there is neither *"then"* nor *"now"*. Exactly: there is even NO NOW at all! Life has no speed. Life has no time. Life HAPPENS. To say it with Alan Watts again:

"Everything is connected"

"HAPPENESS" INSTEAD OF HAPPINESS & HOLINESS

YOU ARE AN INFINITE INSIDE JOB. INFINITY HAS GOT NO SECRET OUTSIDE. YOU CANNOT KILL YOURSELF TO REACH ANY HOLY OUTSIDE. YOU CANNOT SHOOT A HOLE, YOU SHOT JUST THROUGH THE EMPTINESS OF YOUR PROJECTION. THE WHOLE MOMENT CONSISTS OF EVERY-THING THAT IS YOUR EMPTY IDENTITY. YOU ARE THE SELFLESS MOMENT ITSELF. THE MOMENT IS YOUR REAL IDENTITY AS NOBODY. YOU ARE IDENTICAL WITH THE MOMENT. IT HAPPENS ALWAYS NOW. NOW IS NOW. NO MORE *"YOU"* OR *"ME"* BUT JUST THE MOMENT — INCLUDING ANYTHING THAT HAPPENS. YOU HAPPEN NOW. NOBODY LEFT TO BE HOLY OR HAPPY. BE PART OF IT! BE IT! BE! IT IS TRUE...

ZERO MEDITATION

THE SEEKER'S SEARCH OF A DIVINE SEEKING CENTER DIVIDES REAL...IT...Y IN TWO PIECES BUT IT IS NEITHER AN OBJECT NOR AN ILLUSION: EGO FEARS THE INFINITE FLOW BUT IN THE END IT IS JUST UNIVERSE MAKING LOVE WITH ITSELF THRU YOUR NOTHINGNESS AND THIS HAPPENS A B S O L U T E L Y RIGHT NOW!

As long as you search the seeker you observe the observer believing that *"consciousness"* (the so-called *"true self"* or religiously the *"source"* or romantically the *"soul")* should be something different than EVERYTHING THAT HAPPENS. Ego fears the infinite flow (the stream of consciousness!) thru its own emptiness: the world is neither an object (as there is no subject) nor a dream (as there is no awoken *"absolute"* reality beyond THIS) – IT JUST HAPPENS ABSOLUTELY RIGHT NOW! Universe makes love with itself thru your present nothingness...

THERE IS NO *"BEYOND"* OF INFINITY AS IT IS INFINITE. SIMPLE BUT TOO DIFFICULT FOR SIMPLE MINDS: INFINITY AND NOTHINGNESS ARE IDENTICAL...

Not the world is made of consciousness (as if the whole cosmic matter would be a fake, illusion, matrix, maya or at least just a game of God) but consciousness consists of the world: matter becomes aware of itself, THAT'S IT – no god nowhere!

If you believe that life would be an illusion or even just the dream of God, you are separated from THIS TOTAL MOMENT of absolute zeroness!

Everything is an obviously simple game of ego searching itself by believing it would be a divine object of infinity, emptiness, nothingness or the source of life. All that kind of esoteric mindfuck was just invented to keep you a hypnotized slave of meta-physical illusions. THERE IS NOBODY TO WAKE UP – EVERYTHING IS AWAKE! UNIVERSE ITSELF IS THE ETERNAL ESSENCE. THIS IS IT. CELEBRATE LOVE, PEACE AND FREEDOM! HAVE A NICE DAY, HAVE A GREAT TRIP.

The return to reality happens when nobody and nothing is left to return. There is no ego, no center, no source, no essence, no god, no reason, no big bang, no absolute object that gives you any last answer WHAT & WHY life IS – life just *IS...*

BE AWARE - IT IS NOT SCHWER

Is it a typical german phenomena that the same people that *"like"* the descriptions of transspiritual awakening are able to post seriously esoterical mindfuck about *"energy"*, *"essence"*, *"light"* and *"love"* or even *"god"* and *"immortality"* ? There is just one simple reason for that paradox: they are still EGOS that try to define the green grass as something more, bigger, divine and infinite instead of EXPERIEN-CING THE TOTALITY OF EVERYTHING THAT IS WHAT IT IS – nothing *"beyond"* the experience itself! That's life! Nothing needs to be greener than green. The whole universe is just ITSELF. No essence, no energy, no god, no self. Just IT-SELF. The ego produces all these illusions because it hopes to find peace in a greater *"love"* or *"freedom"* than REALITY. Reality is neither a secret nor an object – it is just the flow of consciousness: *"UNIVERSE MAKES LOVE WITH ITSELF ... thru your present nothingness"*. Your illusions of spiritual levels to explain reality exploid in the fire of flow! MOVE YOUR BODY! SHAKE YOUR MIND! BE AWARE – it is not schwer! Your nerves need no ego. They touch the truth directly NOW. Yes. It is true. It is easy. It is YOU: the flow itself...

EGOLESSNESS

Egolessness is no dualism because there is no ego at all existing. Ego is just a word, a thought, a psychic object produced by a thinking that believes to be *"something"* different than the body with all its senses. But your ability to think is indeed just a result of your sensual impressions combined with a neurobiological complexity of your basic being in a human condition. The world is same as the so-called ego not a dualistic thing but infinite so that there is no opposite of the world that could be called *"transcendence"* by religious people or *"nothingness"* by spiritual seekers. Their hyper reflections are in a shocking simple way separated from their direct experiences of life.

ANCIENT GOAL

The ancient goal of yoga had never to do with fakeyoga fitness poses in perfect landscape situations but becoming free of any goal by losing your ego. Any damn pose in any moment (sitting on a toilet, standing in a train, watching tv, working at the computer) is the perfect situation to feel yourself consisting of the whole – no need to search for nothing!

MINDLESSNESS

Your ego wants to be a calm candle flame in a windless place but indeed such an unwavering place does not exist at all. That silly hope is just an illusion of your ego that tries hard to ignore the beauty of itself made of the wind! Each moment, each thought and each feeling of BEING IDENTICAL (not *one with something* but being zero yourself) enlightens your mindless mind to be a wave of the infinite empty ocean!

GREATEST MISTAKE

The typical attitude of all spiritual seekers to believe *"i am neither my body nor my mind"* is THE greatest mistake of the whole yoga scene as it means to stick to the hope of a holy self/soul BEYOND the dualism that shall be free from body+mind. But the truth is indeed that there is NO SELF/SOUL AT ALL and the real last enlightenment is the awakening into a conscious feeling of everything WHAT IS RIGHT NOW as your real i.

NO SECRET ABOUT NO SECRET

No ego no person no identity no searching for truth or emptiness nobody to believe in a secret even not in a secret *"that there is no secret"* – people play people but the grass is green anyway without questioning itself. Universe cannot ask itself *"why"* IT EXISTS as it has no ego to look at itself from outside. YOU ARE NOT OUTSIDE AS WELL: YOU ARE THE *"YOU"* in any aspect that recognizes itself. Pure existence. An absolute feeling!

NO BACKGROUND AT ALL

We finished our research project about the german scene of spiritual seekers now. Some european friends say that our description of TRANSSPIRITUALITY (a *"spiritual"* attitude beyond all beliefs, concepts, methods, projections and hopes of the ego) would be totally new and a kind of revolution but we know well on which *"groundless ground"* we stand: if you read for example ALAN WATTS you find transspirituality already prepared in beautiful words! And nowadays Jed McKenna and Jeff Foster think and feel and touch universe and existence in a similar way. In Germany most *"spiritual seekers"* that want to overcome religious systems just exchange them for other traditions (Buddhism or Advaita) but still believe in becoming *"enlightened"* or *"awaken"* by practising any method to improve their ego under pressure of their longing for truth. But the very sad truth about all that longing for freedom is that they still stick to their egos as a central reality in which they collect all their transpersonal illusions. People that lost their ego don't talk any longer about anything (except Jim Carrey) because they simply have no more concept or method to sell. They are no more gurus, teachers, coaches – but free for their own infinite life. We started our research project about transspirituality in order to FIND words for WHY you lose all words in general (definitions, interpretations, projections) when you need no longer an ego as your center but drop into the FLOW of reality itself as the one and only REAL ABSOLUTE truth without divine background.

The human civilization invented two main dualistic mistakes: 1st its belief in a metaphysical center of each body that shall be divine (infinite, empty, holy) and 2nd its belief in an ego that tries to become identical with that center called soul or God. All problems in the world are the result of this dualism that separates everything from each other (and from itself) instead of feeling the natural flow in which everything is made of everything else in each moment. This is true nondual awareness.

SAND DROPPING

this drop of sand is
no drop and the light
of this drop is no light
to see there is an action
between nothing called
movement but no objects
to save in our mind that
is no object as well
but a movement of
some senses that
happen just as a
happening of
nothingness

AND DOESN'T END

there is no i
but the concrete
body in motion the
body is self-confident
the body is aware of
the body there is
no END but just
the infinite AND
in my dreams i
dream that i am
dreaming a crazy
dream in reality i
realize that i am
realizing a crazy
reality i am
always myself

BLESS AND LESS

i do what i think
i think what i feel
i feel what i am
i am what i see
i see what i think
i think what i feel
i feel what i do
i do what i am
i am what i do

ZERO MEDITATION

no special emotion
to feel the whole
no special thought
to believe all senses
no special movement
to get in touch with
the meaning of
life because i
am made
of that

NO COSMIC COMPASS

there is no soul of no matter no
cosmic energy that develops into
a new divine force of a pretended
person as an agent of god because
infinity needs no god to explain itself
and no intuition to handle with any
anything there is simply that field of
reality that consists of all elements
that are identical with the emptiness
that does not exist at all if something
is able to talk about itself it has to use
a silent language without any letters
because this is this and that is that

Dedicated to Werner Ablass
(1949-2018, R.I.P.)

BE KEEN ON ITS BIKINI

the grain of sand is yellow
the blade of grass is green
the wings of swallows can
be blue but if your tongue
can swallow on what your
ego was dead keen you'll
understand nobody does
but only grains and grass

S E E (K) I N G P E R S O N
[LAST MINDLESS MEDITATION]

who is that person who seeks
itself as if the mirror showed a
different face than your own

who has the ability to reflect
the alertness of existence but
sticks to that stupid belief in a

god or nothingness beyond
your face and your body your
ego separates your seeing self-

confidence that is just a great
feeling of being an infinite wave
consisting of the empty ocean

*"God is nothing
but the power
of the universe
to organize itself."*

Lee Smolin

*"But, as Douglas E. Harding has
pointed out, we tend to think of
this planet as a life-infested rock,
which is as absurd as thinking of
the human body as a cell infested
skeleton. Surely all forms of life,
including man, must be under-
stood as 'symptoms' of the earth,
the solar system, and the galaxy
in which case we cannot escape
the conclusion that the
galaxy is intelligent."*

Alan Watts

This was the extended 5th book

ZERO
MEDITATION
No need to meditate –
life happens anyway !

© www.Zero2go.de

Cover photo by James Roblee
Back cover photo by Umer
Sayyam on Unsplash

All articles and books by
the League of Empty Ones:

www.urruhe.de
www.uryoga.de
www.nullyoga.de
www.antiyoga.de
www.zeroyoga.de
www.relaxyoga.de
www.burnoutyoga.de

Email: *ligaderleeren@gmail.com*